This book belongs to

_____

...a girl after God's own heart.

A JOURNEY THROUGH JAMES

Living
Your
Faith

ELIZABETH
GEORGE

HARVEST
kids™

HARVEST HOUSE PUBLISHERS
EUGENE, OREGON

LIVING YOUR FAITH
Copyright © 2017 Elizabeth George
Published by Harvest House Publishers
Eugene, Oregon 97408
www.harvesthousepublishers.com

ISBN 978-0-7369-6441-8 (pbk.)
ISBN 978-0-7369-6442-5 (eBook)

Contents

A Note Just for You

Hi there!

I'm Elizabeth, and I'm so glad to meet you! And I'm so glad you are holding this book in your hands. I cannot tell you how excited I am that you and I are going to go on a journey together through the book of James.

As you prepare to make this exciting trip, here's a little checklist to get you started on your adventure of living your faith.

Open your heart...

...**to your friends.** It will be so neat to go on this adventure with your best friends! The more girls you get together, the more fun your adventure will be. And don't forget to ask your mom if she would like to go through the book with you.

...**and pray.** Ask Jesus to help you realize how much He loves you. Also ask Him to help you understand what it means to be a girl after His own heart.

Open your book...

...**and dive into the Bible!** I have included the entire Bible text of the book of James so you can easily follow along and answer the questions in each chapter. Everything you need is here—except your favorite pen or pencil. Since this is a Bible study, feel free to underline verses, circle words, make notes to yourself, and even sketch, draw, or doodle. Do whatever helps you better understand the meaning of a verse or passage of Scripture.

At the end of each chapter in this book, you will discover four fun and helpful ways to seal God's truths into your heart and make them part of your daily life as a girl after God's own heart:

- ❤ **A Look Inside Your Heart** focuses on your heart because that's where your attitudes are formed, your decisions are made, and your words come from.

- ❤ **A Heart Checkup** shows you what's happening in your heart and make decisions for change.

- ❤ **A Prayer to Pray** will help you talk to God about your desire to grow in your relationship with Him.

- ❤ **Gems from James** are key verses that will help you remember the important points of that chapter.

Are you ready to let the fun begin? I am! As you read, please remember that I wrote every word with you in my mind and in my heart, and every page of this book is covered with my prayers for *you*. I've had you in my heart for months as I sit here in my office studying the awesome book of James, thinking about you, praying for you, and writing to you.

I've also tried hard to imagine you at home—wherever that

is, whether it's in a city apartment or a suburban home or a farmhouse. And I've tried to picture you in your room or space and with your family. When I say that I consider you to be a friend, even though we haven't met in person, I mean it!

Soooo—ready...set...here we go!

In Jesus' great and amazing love,
Your friend and sister in Christ,

Elizabeth George

Tough Times

JAMES 1:1-12

1 James, a servant of God and of the Lord Jesus Christ, To the twelve tribes scattered among the nations: Greetings.

2 Consider it pure joy, my brothers and sisters, whenever you face trials of many kinds,

3 because you know that the testing of your faith produces perseverance.

4 Let perseverance finish its work so that you may be mature and complete, not lacking anything.

5 If any of you lacks wisdom, you should ask God, who gives generously to all without finding fault, and it will be given to you.

6 But when you ask, you must believe and not doubt, because the one who doubts is like a wave of the sea, blown and tossed by the wind.

7 That person should not expect to receive anything from the Lord.

⁸ Such a person is double-minded and unstable in all they do.

⁹ Believers in humble circumstances ought to take pride in their high position.

¹⁰ But the rich should take pride in their humiliation—since they will pass away like a wild flower.

¹¹ For the sun rises with scorching heat and withers the plant; its blossom falls and its beauty is destroyed. In the same way, the rich will fade away even while they go about their business.

¹² Blessed is the one who perseveres under trial because, having stood the test, that person will receive the crown of life that the Lord has promised to those who love him.

Don't you just love getting a letter or note in the mail? Sure, receiving text messages and emails is fun. But nothing is as personal and exciting as something written by hand on special note paper or a card in an envelope sent with love through the mail to you. Wow! That takes a lot of time, love, thought, and care...and even some money. That means someone *really* loves you and thinks about you a lot!

Well, my new friend, the book of James in the Bible was an actual letter. It was written by James to Jewish believers who were scattered in many countries. These folks needed LOTS of encouragement because they were suffering tough times.

Before you start reading James's letter, read verse 1 and meet the author. How does James, the writer of the book of James, describe himself?

"a _____ of _____ and of the

_____ _____ _____ "

Just a note: Be sure to read Mark 6:3 in your Bible. There you will discover that James was Jesus' half-brother. Can you imagine growing up with an older brother who was perfect? Who never sinned? Who possessed all the wisdom of the ages?

Now that you've met the author of the book of James, what about *your* trials and tests? I'm sure you have your share of tough times! In fact, tough times are a fact of life. Jesus told us, "In this world you will have trouble" (John 16:33). Do you ever wonder, "What am I supposed to do in tough times? What am I supposed to do with my problems?"

Well, you'll be happy to hear that James has some lessons and great advice for dealing with your tough times and trials. Read on!

Learning to Count

In school you learned how to add up a column of numbers— and hopefully get the right answer! Well, as we read verse 2, James tells us, "Consider it pure joy, my brothers and sisters, whenever you face trials of many kinds." The New King James Version says "Count it all joy." When you "count" or add up your sufferings and problems and disappointments, what does James say is the correct answer in verse 2?

"Consider [or count] it _____ _____."

Read verse 2 again and think about the word "many," as in "trials of many kinds." No one wants to face and deal with even one trial! And yet James speaks of many kinds of trials. Maybe you have already experienced several kinds of trials, like...

   a tough decision to do the right thing

   a tragedy in your family

   a serious illness or accident

   facing a mean girl every day at school

   struggling with a difficult subject in school
   (like math or English)

Well, here's some very good news! God does not ask you or any of His people to understand our trials. But He does want us to trust Him and His wisdom and His plan for us. When you do this—when you trust God with your problems—you will find joy in Him, joy in His promises, and joy in His perfect will for your wonderful, special, unique life!

Count Your Blessings

One reason I love the book of James is that it has a lot of lists that help us with our daily trials and challenges. In James 1:3-12 you'll see a list of benefits or blessings or lessons that come from going through trials.

Blessing #1 (verse 3) . . . . Perseverance

" ____ you know that the _____ of _____

_____ produces [or develops] _____."

"Perseverance" is a long word that describes the strength God is building in you when you face tough times. God is right there with you to help you! Perseverance gives you what you need to hang in there until you make it through your problem, until you make it to the end.

Do you know the children's story called The Little Engine That Could? You probably remember that the engine had a tough time pulling the train up steep hills. But he persevered. As he chugged along, he kept saying, "I think I can, I think I can, I think I can, I think I can."

My friend, God gives you His power and grace so you can say, "I *know* I can make it through this problem"—because He is producing perseverance in you.

Blessing #2 (verse 4) . . . . Spiritual Growth

"Let perseverance _____ its _____

so that you may be _____ and _____,

not lacking _____."

Has anyone—maybe a parent or older brother or sister— ever said to you, "Why don't you just grow up?" Or asked, "When are you going to grow up?" Or maybe they just teased you by saying, "Grow up!" Well, James is telling us that when we let perseverance finish its work in us, we grow up spiritually. When you do your work chores over and over, or when you finish your homework over and over, or when you practice your instrument or sport over and over, you are experiencing the blessing of becoming

"mature and

complete,

not lacking anything."

Blessing #3 (verse 5) . . . . Wisdom

"If any of you lacks _____, you should

ask _____, who gives generously to _____

without finding _____, and it will be _____

to _____."

If you're like most people, you need wisdom just about every time you turn around! When someone says or does something that hurts you, you need wisdom to know what to do or say—or what *not* to do or say! When you are invited to go somewhere or do something that your parents would not approve of, or when you're not sure what to do, you need wisdom to know how to answer. You need wisdom for so many things—and you always will. And don't forget, you can always ask your parents what to do about your problems.

God knows you need help, and He enjoys giving it to you. As verse 5 tells you, all you have to do is

_____!

Living Your Faith

When you ask, your blessing will be wisdom that comes from God—which is always perfect.

Before you go on to Blessing #4, read the verses below and check when you are done.

___ verses 6-8, which tell you to **believe God** and trust Him.

___ verses 9-11, which explain that all Christians can **be thankful** that God loves them, no matter whether they are poor or rich.

Blessing #4 (verse 12)

Wow! We began with perseverance...and we are ending with perseverance. When you stand strong through your trials and tough times and don't give in when you are tempted, what happens (verse 12)?

"_____ is the one who _____

under _____ because, having stood the _____,

that person will _____ the crown of _____

that the _____ has _____ to those

who _____ him."

Just a note: When James says we will "receive the crown of life," he is describing heaven.

A LOOK INSIDE YOUR HEART

Glance back through the advice James gives you in the 12 verses included in this lesson about tough times. Think about the epic promise in verse 12. Isn't it amazing to realize that as a child of God, you have a rich heritage? As a child of God, you—yes, you!—can look forward to being with Jesus in heaven, where there will be...

> no tough times,
>
> no more death,
>
> no sorrow,
>
> no crying, and
>
> no more pain.

In fact, God Himself will be with you and be your God. And God will wipe away every tear from your eyes. (You can read about this in Revelation 21:3-4 in your Bible.)

No matter what tough times and trials you are struggling with, you are special and loved by God! I really like these words and hang on to them in tough times:

> "What you have in your heart...
> matters to God and
> endures for eternity."[1]

A HEART CHECKUP

Read verse 1 again. Do you think of yourself as a servant? (Circle one.)

Yes   No   Sometimes

Write down one thing you can do to be more like James as you serve God, serve Jesus, and serve those at home.

I can help..._____

_____

_____

Write a sentence or two that describes how you usually act when you have trials—when someone is mean and hurts your feelings, when you don't get what you want, or when you are sick.

_____

_____

_____

_____

_____

What good advice do you learn in verse 5?

_____

_____

_____

What exciting truth do you learn in verse 5 about God's response to your prayers?

_____

_____

_____

After reading James 1:1-12, how can these verses help you live out your faith? Or put another way, how should you act when things don't go the way you want and you are tempted to act badly. Write them here.

I need to... _____

_____

_____

_____

_____

A PRAYER TO PRAY

Lord Jesus, You already know I've got problems! Help me to face them and to persevere through them. I want to grow up in my love for You and my family. Teach me how to find joy as I deal with my problems and bad attitudes. When I'm confused and worried about what to do, please remind me to pray—to just ASK You for wisdom! I love You, Jesus! Amen.

GEMS FROM JAMES

"Consider it pure joy...whenever you face trials."
James 1:2

"If any of you lacks wisdom, you should ask God."
James 1:5

"Blessed is the one who perseveres under trial."
James 1:12

Trusting God

JAMES 1:13-27

¹³ When tempted, no one should say, "God is tempting me." For God cannot be tempted by evil, nor does he tempt anyone;

¹⁴ but each person is tempted when they are dragged away by their own evil desire and enticed.

¹⁵ Then, after desire has conceived, it gives birth to sin; and sin, when it is full-grown, gives birth to death.

¹⁶ Don't be deceived, my dear brothers and sisters.

¹⁷ Every good and perfect gift is from above, coming down from the Father of the heavenly lights, who does not change like shifting shadows.

¹⁸ He chose to give us birth through the word of truth, that we might be a kind of firstfruits of all he created.

¹⁹ My dear brothers and sisters, take note of this: Everyone should be quick to listen, slow to speak and slow to become angry,

²⁰ because human anger does not produce the righteousness that God desires.

²¹ Therefore, get rid of all moral filth and the evil that is so prevalent and humbly accept the word planted in you, which can save you.

²² Do not merely listen to the word, and so deceive yourselves. Do what it says.

²³ Anyone who listens to the word but does not do what it says is like someone who looks at his face in a mirror

²⁴ and, after looking at himself, goes away and immediately forgets what he looks like.

²⁵ But whoever looks intently into the perfect law that gives freedom, and continues in it—not forgetting what they have heard, but doing it—they will be blessed in what they do.

²⁶ Those who consider themselves religious and yet do not keep a tight rein on their tongues deceive themselves, and their religion is worthless.

²⁷ Religion that God our Father accepts as pure and faultless is this: to look after orphans and widows in their distress and to keep oneself from being polluted by the world.

Millions and millions of people around the world know about God. They know lots of facts and truths and stories about Him. For example, He created the universe and everybody in it. He did loads of miracles.

He gave us the Ten Commandments. He is called God, the Father. He is in heaven and rules over all.

But knowing about God and trusting God are two completely different things. To learn more about what it means to trust God and live out your faith, take a look at these truths about Him that come straight from the Bible.

God Is Special

God is in His very own special category. We learn about Him in the Bible, where He shares truths about Himself. What two truths do you learn about Him in James 1, verse 13?

"...God cannot be _____ by _____,

nor does he _____ anyone."

These two truths mean that when you are tempted, don't blame God. If you give in to temptation and choose to sin and do what you know is wrong, admit it. Don't blame God. As verse 13 tells us, "When tempted, no one should say, 'God is tempting me.'"

Take a look at the excuses below and check the ones you have used:

____"It's the other person's fault."

____"I couldn't help it."

____"Everybody's doing it."

____"It was just a mistake."

____"Nobody's perfect."

____"I didn't know it was wrong."

____"The devil made me do it."

____"I was pressured into it."[2]

What can you do to stop blaming other people and stop giving in to temptation to do wrong things? The answer: Turn to God *before* you make a wrong choice or do the wrong thing! After all, "God is our refuge and strength, a very present help in trouble" (Psalm 46:1 NKJV).

God watches over you. And He is "very present." He is right there with you, all the time—every second and every step, all day and all night. His job is to protect you, give you strength, help you, and guide you. Your job is to turn to Him for His help—for His protection, wisdom, and strength—every time you are tempted. You can definitely trust Him—always.

The next time you are tempted, turn to God. Call on Him right away—before you do or say anything else. Then ask Him, "God, what is the right thing to do?"

Learning More About God

You already know from verse 13 that "God cannot be tempted by evil, nor does he tempt anyone." Now verses 14-18 show us how a temptation leads to sin. Verse 14 tells us,

"...each person is _____ when they are

_____ _____ by their

own _____ _____ and enticed."

Living Your Faith

Verse 15 tells us,

"...after desire has _____, it
gives birth to _____, and sin, when it is _____-
_____, gives birth to _____."

Verse 16 gives us a command. Write it here:

"Don't be _____."

In these verses (14, 15, and 16), James is warning you and all believers not to be deceived. How are believers deceived? They start thinking things that aren't true, like...

"God isn't real."

"God doesn't care about me."

"God really can't help me."

But God *is* real, and He *does* care about you! In fact, He cares for you more than any other person in the world cares for you. He loves you so much that He sent His Son to die on a cross for your sins. And He not only **wants** to help you, He also **can** help you...and He does.

Remember these truths. Hide them in your heart and use them daily. God hears your prayers and your cries for help (look again at James 1:5)...and He answers them. The first thing to do in every situation is to pray. You don't have to kneel or bow down. And you don't have to speak out loud. Just talk to God in your heart. You can simply say to Him, "Help me, Lord!"

Verse 17 teaches us that God is the source of everything that is good. Whatever you have that is good and perfect comes from Him. He can give only good and perfect gifts because He is good and perfect! How is God described in verse 17?

"Every good and perfect gift is from _____,

coming down from the _____ of the

heavenly _____, who does not _____

like shifting _____."

Verse 18 refers to the people James was writing to.

"He chose to give us _____ through the

word of _____, that we might be a kind of

_____ of all he _____."

The people reading James's handwritten letter were the very first group of believers after Jesus died, rose from the grave, and ascended into heaven. James wrote that they were "a kind of firstfruits of all he created." In other words, they were the first children in God's new family.

There's a LOT of information about God in verse 18! The New Century Version of the Bible ends verse 18 by saying God wanted us to be "the most important of all the things he made." Wow! That's special!

Some Awesome Advice

Prepare yourself for some really practical, easy-to-understand information you need every single day! Read verse 19 and list the three awesome ways to keep out of trouble, make right choices, and live as God's child.

"Everyone should be quick to _____,
slow to _____ and slow to _____
_____."

An ancient teacher named Zeno put it this way:

"We have two ears, but only one mouth,
that we may hear more and speak less."

According to verse 20, why must anger be controlled?

"Because human _____ does not produce
the _____ that God _____."

Here's an exercise for you. Tomorrow, keep a list of how many times you were angry...

in your heart,

in your attitude,

in the way you treated someone,

in your words,

in your actions, or

in a complete, full-out blow-up or tantrum.

Now that you know the truth of verse 20—that your anger does not produce the good behavior God desires—what are some things you can do the next time you are tempted to give in to anger? Maybe count to ten? What else? Write them here:

_____

_____

_____

_____

Getting Rid of What's Bad

Has your father or mother ever asked you to clean out your closet or your dresser drawers and get rid of all the old stuff and junk inside them? Well, that's exactly what God, your heavenly Father, is asking you to do in verse 21. He wants you to...

"...get rid of all moral _____ and the

_____ that is so prevalent."

> **Just a note:** "Prevalent" means common and commonly accepted.

Once you have thrown out all the old, yucky stuff in your life, what should you put in its place? Verse 21 says,

"...humbly accept the _____ planted in _____,

which can _____ _____."

Read verse 22 and write out God's homework for you—what you are to do, and what you are not to do.

"Do not merely _____ to the

_____, and so _____ yourselves.

Do _____ it _____."

James gives you a great word picture of those who do not do what the Word of God says. What is the picture in verses 23 and 24? "Anyone who listens to the word but does not do what it says is like someone who...

...looks at his _____ in a _____ and,

after looking at himself, _____ _____

and immediately forgets what he _____ like."

What does the end of verse 25 say happens to someone who does what the Word of God says to do?

"—they will be _____ in what _____

_____."

Be sure to read verses 26 and 27 and check here when you are done ___. They are a good reminder to...

keep a tight hold on your tongue,

keep your eye out for those who need help, and

keep yourself pure from the world.

A LOOK INSIDE YOUR HEART

In this lesson, we've looked at a lot of truths and instructions about trusting God. As you continue getting to know God better, and as you keep growing in your faith in Him, you will learn more and more about what God wants for you.

I am praying for you and your heart. I want you to fall in love with God and His Word. Make Him your first thought when you wake up. If Mom wakes you up, say, "Okay, Mom, I'm getting up"—and then let your very next thought be a heart prayer to God. Express your love to Him. Give Him your day. Ask Him to help you live for Him, to live your faith. Fill your mind and heart with thoughts of His Word. Praise Him for who He is, and thank Him for what He's done. And don't forget to include the epic truths you have learned about Him in just this first chapter of James:

— God is available to help you through your tough times.

— God is your refuge and strength, a very present help in trouble.

— God hears the prayers of your heart...and answers them.

— God will help you to follow Him with all your heart and to do what His Word says.

— God will help you clean out your heart and do away with what is ugly and evil, and He will create a pure heart in you. (Read Psalm 51:10 in your Bible.)

Living Your Faith

Surely you know by now that you can trust God because He can and will do all of this for you—and more!

A HEART CHECKUP

What good advice did you learn in verse 19?

_____

_____

_____

Write out at least one way you can...

—keep a tight hold on your tongue (verse 26),

_____

_____

_____

—keep your eye out for those who need help (verse 27), and

_____

_____

—keep yourself pure from the world, from doing what is wrong (verse 27).

_____

_____

_____

A PRAYER TO PRAY

Father, I know I spend too much time worrying about whether I look okay. Help me to see myself the way You see me—beautiful inside and out. You have made me a girl after Your own heart! As Your love overflows in me, help me share that love with others by controlling my tongue and changing my behavior. I want to honor You and live out my faith by obeying Your guidelines. I want my heart to be like Yours, and I want to do what Your Word says. I love You, God! Amen.

GEMS FROM JAMES

"Be quick to listen,
slow to speak and
slow to become angry."
James 1:19

"Do not merely listen to the word...
Do what it says."
James 1:22

Playing Favorites

JAMES 2:1-13

¹ My brothers and sisters, believers in our glorious Lord Jesus Christ must not show favoritism.

² Suppose a man comes into your meeting wearing a gold ring and fine clothes, and a poor man in filthy old clothes also comes in.

³ If you show special attention to the man wearing fine clothes and say, "Here's a good seat for you," but say to the poor man, "You stand there" or "Sit on the floor by my feet,"

⁴ have you not discriminated among yourselves and become judges with evil thoughts?

⁵ Listen, my dear brothers and sisters: Has not God chosen those who are poor in the eyes of the world to be rich in faith and to inherit the kingdom he promised those who love him?

⁶ But you have dishonored the poor. Is it not the rich who are exploiting you? Are they not the ones who are dragging you into court?

⁷ Are they not the ones who are blaspheming the noble name of him to whom you belong?

⁸ If you really keep the royal law found in Scripture, "Love your neighbor as yourself," you are doing right.

⁹ But if you show favoritism, you sin and are convicted by the law as lawbreakers.

¹⁰ For whoever keeps the whole law and yet stumbles at just one point is guilty of breaking all of it.

¹¹ For he who said, "You shall not commit adultery," also said, "You shall not murder." If you do not commit adultery but do commit murder, you have become a lawbreaker.

¹² Speak and act as those who are going to be judged by the law that gives freedom,

¹³ because judgment without mercy will be shown to anyone who has not been merciful. Mercy triumphs over judgment.

You probably already know about favoritism from your experiences at school, in your neighborhood, and maybe even in your family. You can tell when someone is clearly the teacher's pet! Or when someone is treated with great respect—or just a little. An author who writes books about leadership and trust wrote, "Playing favorites is one of the most damaging problems in any group of people."[3]

This problem has evidently been around for a long time, because the next important lesson James has for us is about showing favoritism, or partiality.

Accepting Others

There's no doubt that playing favorites causes mountains of problems, hurt feelings, and broken friendships. It's no wonder that James boldly says in James 2, verse 1, "Believers in our glorious Lord Jesus Christ must not show favoritism." It's like James is saying, "Do not show partiality! Do not play favorites!" In plain language, he is telling us, "Stop it!"

We are surrounded by all kinds of discrimination or favoritism based on people's...

money or possessions,

race or religious practices,

personality or intelligence,

home or neighborhood,

family reputation, or

outward appearance.

In the previous chapter, you read that Christians are to help take care of orphans and widows (James 1:27). When James was writing, these two groups of people were often overlooked and received no help. Instead of taking care of anyone who was in need, people were turning their attention, time, and help toward only those who were wealthy, good-looking, popular, or powerful.

In this lesson, James addresses partiality and favoritism in the church by making up a story about two men.

In verse 2, how is the first man described?

"a man wearing a _____ _____ and _____ clothes"

How is the second man described in verse 2?

"a poor _____ in _____ _____ clothes"

In verse 3, what did the people say to the man who wore nice clothes?

"Here's a _____ _____ for _____."

In verse 3, what did the people say to the poor man?

"'You _____ _____,' or '_____ on the _____ by my _____.'"

In verse 4, James ends his story by saying to those who treated the rich man well but disrespected the poor man,

"...have you not discriminated among _____ and become _____ with _____ thoughts?"

Topsy-Turvy

It's amazing how God takes the ways we naturally think and behave and turns them upside down! For instance, most people want to be better than everyone else. They want better everything—better clothes, grades, popularity, and more! That's natural.

But in the Bible, God shows us that the way up is down. In other words, we don't become better people by stepping on others in a race to get to the top. Oh, no! The way up in God's eyes is down. It's our humility that counts with God.

Now take a look at a few other topsy-turvy truths as you continue on in James 2. In verse 5, James points out that God has "chosen those who are poor in the eyes of the world...

to be _____ in _____ and to inherit

the _____ he promised those who

_____ _____."

But the people who are reading James's letter had not realized this wonderful truth. Instead, James says in verse 6,

"But you have _____ the

_____."

James next shares a list of evil acts that the rich people practiced. He asks a series of questions that condemn those who mistreat the poor. In verse 6 and 7, James asks,

"Is it not the _____ who are exploiting you? Are they not the ones who are _____ you into court?" Are they not the ones who are _____ the noble _____ of him to whom you _____?"

Just a note: The word "exploiting" means to take advantage of someone, and "blaspheming" means to curse someone.

The Royal Law

James next refers to "the royal law found in Scripture." When you are wondering what is right and what is wrong, this law will guide you. Write out what James says about "the royal law" in verse 8:

"If you really _____ the _____ _____ found in Scripture, 'Love your _____ as yourself,' you are doing _____."

Then James says in verse 9,

"But if you show _____, you _____

and are _____ by the _____

as lawbreakers."

In verses 10-13, James concludes by letting readers know that sin is sin—if we break even one of God's laws, we are just as guilty as if we had broken all of them. James ends his message on partiality and favoritism with a truth we should never forget. Write out verse 13, which contains James's conclusion and final statement.

"... judgment without _____ will be shown

to _____ who has not been _____

Mercy _____ over _____."

My friend, the important thing to remember about sin and judgment, and about mercy and the royal law of love, is this: God wants you to show mercy—to be merciful. He wants you to be like Him, for "the Lord your God is a merciful God." (That's what the Bible says in Deuteronomy 4:31 NRSV.)

Your acts of mercy and your kindness are proof that you follow Christ. As a child of God and a believer in Christ, you have experienced God's mercy. Therefore you can and should be merciful toward others.

The next time you judge another person or talk about them or snub them because they are different, remember these truths about favoritism.

Why is showing favoritism wrong?

— It is the opposite of what Jesus told us to do.

— It results from evil thoughts.

— It insults people made in God's image.

— It comes from selfish motives.

— It goes against the Bible's definition of love.

— It shows a lack of mercy to those less fortunate.

— It is sin.[4]

A LOOK INSIDE YOUR HEART

I just love this true confession written by a teen who looked inside his heart and learned to accept others and not play favorites or show partiality. As you read it, ask yourself, "Am I an unfair judge?"

Unfair Judges

A new kid came to our school last year, and he was a little on the heavy side. No one gave him a chance to show what kind of person he was; instead, everyone judged him by his weight. Unfortunately, I did too. Later in the year, many of us got to know him better, and he turned out to be really cool. I felt so guilty about the way we acted earlier, and I wish we hadn't judged him because of his appearance.

I'm sure everybody has treated someone unfairly at one time or another. And most of us can be kind of shallow and sometimes judge people by how they look. But God is never shallow. He cares about all of us—not because of what we look like, but because of who we are…

You can thank God for the unique way he's made you and for the way he's made other people too.

—Spencer[5]

A HEART CHECKUP

You're a girl, so you probably take a look in the mirror before you leave the house for school, church, or just about any activity, right? Well, in Colossians 3:12 God tells us exactly what we should be wearing—what is beautiful in His eyes:

"Therefore, as God's chosen people, holy and dearly loved, as the elect of God, holy and beloved, clothe yourselves with

> compassion,
> kindness,
> humility,
> gentleness and
> patience."

Make it a point to pray and put on the garments Colossians 3:12 mentions. Which of these beautiful pieces of clothing would you like to try on first? In other words, which godly character quality can you start wearing right now? Name it here:

_____

_____

What one thing will you do to put this godly character quality into action in your life as you live out your faith?

_____

_____

A PRAYER TO PRAY

Jesus, You are "our glorious Lord Jesus Christ" [James 2:1], and I thank You that You love me—yes, me!—just as I am. Thank You for helping me to love all people the same, to show respect to those who have less than others, and to be merciful to those who need some help. I want to live out Your royal law of love and love others as I love myself. And boy, do I ever need Your help and Your love to do this! I love You, Jesus! Amen.

GEMS FROM JAMES

"Do not hold the faith of our Lord Jesus Christ,
the Lord of glory, with partiality."
James 2:1 NKJV

"If you really keep the royal law found in Scripture,
'Love your neighbor as yourself,' you are doing right."
James 2:8

"If you show partiality, you commit sin."
James 2:9 NKJV

Be the Real Thing

JAMES 2:14-26

14 What good is it, my brothers and sisters, if someone claims to have faith but has no deeds? Can such faith save them?

15 Suppose a brother or a sister is without clothes and daily food.

16 If one of you says to them, "Go in peace; keep warm and well fed," but does nothing about their physical needs, what good is it?

17 In the same way, faith by itself, if it is not accompanied by action, is dead.

18 But someone will say, "You have faith; I have deeds."

Show me your faith without deeds, and I will show you my faith by my deeds.

19 You believe that there is one God. Good! Even the demons believe that—and shudder.

20 You foolish person, do you want evidence that faith without deeds is useless?

²¹ Was not our father Abraham considered righteous for what he did when he offered his son Isaac on the altar?

²² You see that his faith and his actions were working together, and his faith was made complete by what he did.

²³ And the scripture was fulfilled that says, "Abraham believed God, and it was credited to him as righteousness," and he was called God's friend.

²⁴ You see that a person is considered righteous by what they do and not by faith alone.

²⁵ In the same way, was not even Rahab the prostitute considered righteous for what she did when she gave lodging to the spies and sent them off in a different direction?

²⁶ As the body without the spirit is dead, so faith without deeds is dead.

The saying "You can tell a tree by its fruit" is definitely true—and helpful!

It's amazing that there are so many different kinds of trees. And we don't always know exactly what kind of tree we are looking at. But once a tree bears fruit and we can *see* the fruit, we can *know* exactly what kind of tree it is. An apple tree bears apples. A walnut tree bears walnuts. It's that simple!

In the book of James, you will discover the same is true of a person's faith—and that includes your faith. It's super easy for anyone to go around saying, "Oh yeah, sure. I believe. I have faith. I'm a Christian." But just *saying* you have faith doesn't mean anything. Genuine faith, faith that is real, always results in fruit—spiritual fruit. When your faith is real and you are living your faith, you can't help but do what God says to do.

Looking for the Real Thing

James, the writer of this letter in the Bible, has a very serious topic to share with his readers—including us! That topic is being the real thing, a true believer in Christ. James, chapter 2, introduces this important subject by asking some questions that grab our attention. As you read them, you will see that they give you some important things to think about—and do something about. Complete James 2:14 here:

Question 1: "What good is it, my brothers and sisters, if someone…

_____ to have _____ but has no

_____?"

Question 2: "Can…

such _____ _____ them?"

That's a lot to think about, isn't it? In fact, entire books have been written to answer these two questions about faith and the fruit it produces. Well, James comes to our rescue. He helps us understand by telling us a story. In his story, a person says they have faith, but their actions don't back up their words. Their actions and deeds do not give any evidence that their faith is real.

Now read through verses 15 and 16. In them James is showing us two kinds of responses to people in need, people who need help. And James ends his examples with a thought-provoking question.

As you are reading, keep in mind that the "brother" or "sister" in these verses is not a sibling, but a brother or sister in Christ. They are fellow believers in Christ.

James begins his story in verses 15-16: "Suppose a brother or a sister is without clothes and daily food. If one of you says to them,

'Go in _____ ; keep _____ and _____ _____ ,' but does nothing about _____ _____ _____ , what _____ _____ it?"

Just to make sure you understand James's message, answer these questions:

In verse 15, who was in need?

_____

_____

Also in verse 15, what did they need?

_____

_____

In verse 16, what did the person *say* to the one in need?

_____

_____

Also in verse 16, what did the person *do* for the one in need?

_____

_____

James tells us the point of his story in verse 17:

"In the same way, faith by _____, if it is

not accompanied by _____, is _____."

It is clear that our faith is not proved by what we say—it is proved by what we do! Real faith overflows with good deeds, with spiritual fruit, like helping a fellow believer in need.

Just like James, the apostle Paul tells us how we are to treat our brothers and sisters in Christ. "As we have opportunity, let us do good to all people, especially to those who belong to the family of believers" (Galatians 6:10). Notice a few important commands the apostle Paul wants us to pay attention to:

Let us do good to _____ _____,

especially to those who _____ to the

_____ of _____."

What kind of good deeds can overflow from **your** genuine faith, **your** love for Jesus? Try this: Make a list of the people in your own family, and then jot down several good things or good deeds you can do for them that would help them out, that would make their day a little better.

Person's Name	My Good Deed
(Example: Mom)	(Example: Help her at mealtime)

John Wesley, a famous preacher from the past, understood the principle of doing good. In fact, he made it a rule for his life and put it in these words:

> "Do all the good you can,
> by all the means you can,
> in all the ways you can,
> in all the places you can,
> at all the times you can,
> to all the people you can,
> as long as ever you can."

I've just about memorized this saying—and you can too. But the most important thing is to do it and live it!

It's a good thing to help or do a good deed. But think about this. In Matthew 5:41, Jesus said, "If anyone forces you to go one mile, go with them two miles." This is usually referred to as "going the extra mile." The next time your parents ask you to help them or to do your work chores, do what they ask. Then, after you've done what they told you to do (that's the "one mile") ask them, "Is there anything else I can do for you?" (And that's the "second mile"!)

Warning! Be prepared for some very surprised reactions...and hope your mom doesn't faint!

Examples of Real Faith

Now read James 2, verses 18-19. Here you meet a person who argues, "You have faith; I have deeds." This person seems to think that faith has nothing to do with good deeds. But James replies that faith and good deeds cannot be separated. Our good deeds demonstrate that we have faith. True faith and good deeds go together.

To those people who think their faith is more important than their good deeds, James declares, "Even the demons believe" in God. Even the demons have faith, but their faith doesn't do them any good.

In verses 20-25, James gives two examples of people in the Bible who proved their faith was the real thing by what they did. The first person is Abraham. In verse 21, what did Abraham do that proved he had faith in God and trusted in God?

"...he offered _____ _____ _____

on the _____."

What does James say in verse 24 after pointing out Abraham's faith and deeds? "You see that a person is considered...

righteous by _____ _____ _____

and not by _____ _____."

In verse 25, James gives another example. This time he introduces a woman named Rahab who proved her faith was real by what she did. What did Rahab do that proved she had faith in God and trusted in God?

"...she gave lodging to the _____ and sent

them off in a _____ _____."

James says in verse 25 that, like Abraham, Rahab was "considered...

righteous for what she _____."

James summarizes his teaching with an illustration in verse 26:

"As the _____ without the _____

is dead, so _____ without _____ is

dead."

A LOOK INSIDE YOUR HEART

We began this chapter with an illustration of a fruit tree. We admitted that until we actually see the fruit on a tree, we cannot really know what kind of tree it is. Well, in the Bible God gives us a list of *spiritual* fruit that shows the whole world that we are the real thing—real followers of Jesus. The fruit of the Spirit proves that we are true Christians, that we belong to God, and that our faith is real.

> "The fruit of the Spirit is love, joy, peace, forbearance, kindness, goodness, faithfulness, gentleness and self-control" (Galatians 5:22-23).

A HEART CHECKUP

Create a "good deeds" list of things you could do (or have done) that show the spiritual fruit of your genuine, for-real faith. As you work on your list, remember it's always good to start at home, with your family. Are you patient with your brothers and sisters? Do you express your love for your family with hugs, help, notes, and love? Are you tender and gentle with others?

When you "walk by the Spirit" (Galatians 5:16) the way God teaches in the Bible, you will exhibit the fruit of the Spirit. Search your heart to see what kind of fruit you are bearing. As you look at the list of the fruit of the Spirit, jot down something you can do to express each of the fruit in your life.

The fruit of the Spirit	How I can show this in my life
Love:	_____
Joy:	_____
Peace:	_____
Forbearance (patience):	_____
Kindness:	_____
Goodness:	_____
Faithfulness:	_____
Gentleness:	_____
Self-control:	_____

As you look at your list, if there were places you had trouble coming up with examples or ideas, don't panic! God loves you and wants to work in your life and help you grow in those areas. Write a note to Him below, asking for His help in any areas you struggle with.

_____

_____

_____

_____

_____

A PRAYER TO PRAY

Dear Father, with all my heart I want to be the real thing! As I read Your Word and see how important my faith and my actions are, I am asking You for Your help. Open my eyes to see people who are in need. Open my hands to do what I can. Open my mouth to speak words that are kind and helpful. Open my heart to care for others the way You care for others...and me! I love you, dear Father above! Amen.

GEMS FROM JAMES

"Faith by itself, if it is not
accompanied by action, is dead."
James 2:17

"A person is considered righteous
by what they do and not by faith alone."
James 2:24

"As the body without the spirit is dead,
so faith without deeds is dead."
James 2:26

Taming Your Tongue

JAMES 3:1-12

1 Not many of you should become teachers, my fellow believers, because you know that we who teach will be judged more strictly.

2 We all stumble in many ways. Anyone who is never at fault in what they say is perfect, able to keep their whole body in check.

3 When we put bits into the mouths of horses to make them obey us, we can turn the whole animal.

4 Or take ships as an example. Although they are so large and are driven by strong winds, they are steered by a very small rudder wherever the pilot wants to go.

5 Likewise, the tongue is a small part of the body, but it makes great boasts. Consider what a great forest is set on fire by a small spark.

6 The tongue also is a fire, a world of evil among the parts of the body. It corrupts the whole body, sets the whole course of one's life on fire, and is itself set on fire by hell.

⁷ All kinds of animals, birds, reptiles and sea creatures are being tamed and have been tamed by mankind,

⁸ but no human being can tame the tongue. It is a restless evil, full of deadly poison.

⁹ With the tongue we praise our Lord and Father, and with it we curse human beings, who have been made in God's likeness.

¹⁰ Out of the same mouth come praise and cursing. My brothers and sisters, this should not be.

¹¹ Can both fresh water and salt water flow from the same spring?

¹² My brothers and sisters, can a fig tree bear olives, or a grapevine bear figs? Neither can a salt spring produce fresh water.

I am sure your parents are excited to see you learn how to do more and more things. They probably encourage you to be better and do better. They try to teach you how to use good manners, how to eat properly, how to meet new people and make friends, and how to behave around adults and carry on a conversation with them.

On and on your parents' efforts go. And that's a good thing! It means they love you and want you to feel comfortable about manners and etiquette and to be able to talk with people without feeling awkward.

But the truth is, you and I will never be perfect. Jesus is the only perfect person who ever lived. He was perfect, which made it possible for Him to pay the penalty for our sins.

Now back to James, chapter 2. What does verse 3 tell you?

"We all _____ in _____ _____."

Are you ready to have some fun? I can never read—or even think about—James, chapter 3, and its many practical lessons without laughing out loud. That's because of a super crazy lesson my two daughters experienced in their student group at church. Pastor Eric was leading the kids in his class through James, chapter 3, and he especially wanted them to learn how awful the words they speak can be.

So off Pastor Eric went to the supermarket, where he made a curious purchase in the fresh meat department: He bought a huge, slimy, blood-red, five-pound cow tongue!

And sure enough, at church on Sunday, Pastor Eric unwrapped the cow tongue and passed it around to everyone in the class. He told the kids to look at it. To smell it. To touch it!

I'm sure you can imagine the responses. "Ugh!" "Gross!" "Nasty!" A few kids even said, "I'm going to throw up!"

I'm guessing Pastor Eric was smiling and fist-pumping in his heart, thinking, "Yes! Point made!" Then he had the group open their Bibles, and they all read and discussed how terrible the tongue is—and the damage their words can do to others. I know my two girls got the message, because I heard them saying "Ugh!" and "Gross!" and making disgusting comments!

Look now for yourself to see what James has to say about the tongue—your tongue and mine—and how we can tame it!

Word Pictures

James is a master at using word pictures to teach God's truths. Write out the first word picture he uses in verse 3.

"...we put bits into the _____ of _____."

And why do we do this?

"...to _____ _____ obey _____."

What is the result?

"...we can turn the _____ _____."

Did you know that an average full-grown, healthy horse weighs about 850 to 1,200 pounds? That's about half a ton! And yet by putting a bit in its mouth, as James says, we can control and "turn the whole animal."

In verse 4, James presents two more word pictures. The first one is about ships. What does James say can drive and steer a huge wind-driven ship?

"...they are steered by a _____ _____ _____ wherever the pilot _____ _____ _____."

Living Your Faith

James applies these word pictures to us in verse 5: "Likewise, the tongue...

"is a _____ _____ of the

body, but it makes _____ _____."

What is the next word picture in verse 5?

"Consider what a _____ forest is set on fire

by a _____ spark."

James continues with the word picture of fire. In verse 6 we learn,

"The tongue also is a _____, a world of _____

among the parts of the _____. It _____

the whole _____, sets the whole _____

of one's _____ on _____, and is itself set

_____ _____ by _____."

In verses 7 and 8, James presents another startling truth about the tongue. He begins by listing things we are able to tame or control. Write out the list found in verse 7: We can tame...

"All kinds of (1)_____,

(2) _____,

(3) _____, and

(4) _____ _____."

Now complete this fact or truth in verse 8: "But no human being can...

_____ the _____."

Why? Because...

"It is a _____ _____,

full of _____ _____."

Ridiculous Examples

James next shares several shocking thoughts or truths in verses 9 and 10. In verse 9 he writes,

"With the tongue we praise our _____ and

_____, and with it we curse _____

_____, who _____ _____ made

in _____ _____."

He summarizes his point in verse 10:

"Out of the same _____ come _____

and _____."

In verse 10, what does James think about the fact that we use our mouths both to praise God and to curse people?

"My brothers and sisters, _____ _____

not _____."

God made every single human being in His own image. That means every single human being is special. Therefore we are not to "curse" people, or put them down, or call them bad names, like "loser" or "stupid" or "idiot." We are to bless people and say good things about them when we talk to them or when we talk about them with someone else.

Examples from Nature

Read the question James asks in verse 11. What is the natural answer to this question?

_____

Now read the next question James asks in verse 12. What is the obvious answer to this question?

_____

James uses these two simple laws of nature to make his point. I trust you answered **no** to the two questions in verses 11 and 12. Fresh water and salt water cannot flow from the same spring, and a fig tree cannot bear olives, and a grapevine cannot bear figs.

My friend, God's message is clear. Only good should come out of the mouth of a person who loves and follows God. Praise and cursing should not come out of the same mouth—and that includes **your** mouth.

A LOOK INSIDE YOUR HEART

In this chapter of James, the Bible teaches us that every person alive—including you and me—has a BIG problem with their mouth and their words. But God's Word also tells us what to do about our tongue—how to tame it. Here are three instructions from God's heart to yours. Underline what these verses tell you to say—and not say—with your tongue.

- ❤ "Do not let any unwholesome talk come out of your mouths, but only what is helpful for building others up according to their needs, that it may benefit those who listen" (Ephesians 4:29).

- ❤ "Whoever would love life and see good days must keep their tongue from evil and their lips from deceitful speech" (1 Peter 3:10).

- ❤ "Set a guard over my mouth, LORD; keep watch over the door of my lips" (Psalm 141:3).

Every day when you wake up, ask God to help you live in a way that pleases Him and helps people. One sure way to do this is with your words. I'm sure you've been hurt by harsh, mean, or untrue words that were spoken to you or shared with someone else. Ask God to help you not to be *that* girl—the girl whose mouth hurts others instead of helping them. These three steps will help you tame your tongue:

> Think before you speak.
> Better yet, pray before you speak!
> And if you get angry, don't say a word.

A HEART CHECKUP

Here's a truth about the mouth: Everything you say comes right out of your heart. In Matthew 15:18, Jesus said, "The things that come out of a person's mouth come from the heart."

And in Luke 6:45, Jesus explained, "A good man brings good things out of the good stored up in his heart, and an evil man brings evil things out of the evil stored up in his heart. For the mouth speaks what the heart is full of."

— Read Luke 6:45 again. Underline every time Jesus used the word "good," and circle every time He used the word "evil." Let Jesus' message sink into your heart.

— Set a personal goal to notice and keep track of what you say and talk about. One way to keep track is to write in a journal each day. Write down some good things you said that helped other people. Also note some things you wish you hadn't said because they really hurt someone. Then ask God to help you speak the right kind of words tomorrow. This will help you realize when you are hurting others with your words and when you are helping others by saying more positive, helpful things—things that bless and encourage others.

— Think about 1 Samuel 23:16: "Saul's son Jonathan went to David...and helped him find strength in God." David and Jonathan were best friends. How can you be this kind of friend...this kind of girl?

A PRAYER TO PRAY

Lord, I truly want to watch my mouth and tame my tongue! I know how it feels to be hurt by something someone says, and I don't want to do that to anyone. I am praying the same prayer King David prayed: "Let the words of my mouth and the meditation of my heart be acceptable in Your sight" (Psalm 19:14 NKJV). Help me, Father. Please give me words that are kind and encourage others, words that help and build others up. I love You, Lord, and I want to love others with my words. Amen.

GEMS FROM JAMES

"Out of the same mouth
come praise and cursing...
This should not be."
James 3:10

Doing What's Right

JAMES 3:13-18

¹³ Who is wise and understanding among you? Let them show it by their good life, by deeds done in the humility that comes from wisdom.

¹⁴ But if you harbor bitter envy and selfish ambition in your hearts, do not boast about it or deny the truth.

¹⁵ Such "wisdom" does not come down from heaven but is earthly, unspiritual, demonic.

¹⁶ For where you have envy and selfish ambition, there you find disorder and every evil practice.

¹⁷ But the wisdom that comes from heaven is first of all pure; then peace-loving, considerate, submissive, full of mercy and good fruit, impartial and sincere.

¹⁸ Peacemakers who sow in peace reap a harvest of righteousness.

Do you write in a diary or keep a journal? I've been journaling ever since I was a girl like you. A journal is a good place to think through the events of your days and the things you are learning. You can write down Bible verses you like and want to remember. You can copy something helpful you read in a book or magazine. You can keep your prayer list there and see how God is answering your requests. What you write in your journal entries gives you material to meditate and reflect on, especially lessons God is teaching you in His Word about living your faith.

As we walked together through chapter 5, "Taming Your Tongue," I hope God's message to you came through loud and clear and settled deep in your heart. God wants us to use our words to help other people and bless them—never to hurt them. Now, as we begin this new chapter, we will learn about **true wisdom**, which helps us say and do what's right. As you will soon discover, there are two very different kinds of wisdom.

Before we begin looking at these two kinds of wisdom, turn back to chapter 1 and read James 1, verse 5. In this verse, James explained how you can obtain wisdom. What did he say to do?

"...ask _____, who _____ generously to

_____ without _____ _____."

And what did James say would happen?

"...it will be _____ to _____."

Now, in James 3:13-18, let's see how James describes the two kinds of wisdom.

Heavenly Wisdom

You already know James likes to dive right into a subject and get straight to the point. What is James's question in verse 13?

"Who is _____ and _____

among _____?"

Verse 13 tells us that those who are wise and understanding will...

"show it by their _____ _____, by

_____ done in the _____

that comes from _____."

In other words, how you act is proof that you possess true wisdom—the kind of wisdom that helps you do what's right.

Look at verses 17 and 18 now and learn about heavenly wisdom. Then we will return to verses 14, 15, and 16 to learn about a very different kind of wisdom.

In verse 17, James calls this kind of wisdom...

"...the wisdom that _____ from _____."

He describes this heavenly wisdom as...

"first of all pure; then _____-_____,

considerate, _____, full of _____
and _____ _____, impartial and
_____."

Imagine for a minute having a necklace with a beautiful pearl on it. Wouldn't that be special? You would probably want to wear it every day. Now, imagine having a necklace with **seven** beautiful pearls strung on it. That would be super incredible! And that's exactly what James is giving to you in verse 17—seven awesome pearls of heavenly wisdom that will make you more beautiful inside and out.

Notice what James mentions first: "The wisdom that comes from heaven is first of all pure." This means **purity** is one of the main characteristics of heavenly wisdom. As we continue getting to know our holy God, learning to live the way He wants us to, and praising and worshipping Him, we will grow in purity.

What does it mean to be pure? Picture a glass of filtered water. It's completely clear and clean—it doesn't have anything else mixed in. Doesn't that sound refreshing?

In the same way, when we live by the wisdom that comes from above...

— we **think** positive and helpful thoughts. Bad and harmful thoughts are filtered out.

— we **act** the way Jesus teaches us to, without mixing in any unloving or destructive behaviors.

Of course, sometimes we make mistakes. Does that mean we can no longer be pure? Not at all! The great news is that when we mess up, God gives us a way to be made clean and pure again. First John 1:9 shows us the way:

> "If we confess our sins, he is faithful and just and will forgive us our sins and purify us from all unrighteousness."

To confess your sin means to agree with God when your thoughts or actions are not pure and pleasing to Him. So when you **think** an impure thought, confess it. When you **say** something impure, confess it. Jesus, the one who died for your sins, is ready to forgive you.

Now back to James. After James names the first pearl—
❤ **purity**—he lists six more beautiful pearls that describe the wisdom that comes from heaven:

- ❤ **peace-loving**—willing to make sacrifices to maintain peace in your relationships

- ❤ **considerate**—gentle, kind, and forgiving, not seeking your own way

- ❤ **submissive**—willing to listen and learn from others and consider what they have to say

- ❤ **full of mercy and good fruits**—compassionate toward others and demonstrating your faith through your actions

- ❤ **impartial**—not playing favorites

- ❤ **sincere**—not being two-faced, pretending, deceiving, or being selfish.

As I look at this list, I'm thinking about the best place to practice these marks of God's wisdom—and that's at home, with those closest to you. The way you live at home shows who you really are. So be this person at home. Bless those you live with. Then walk out your door and do the same and bless others.

In verse 18 James gives the final description of a person who possesses heavenly wisdom. James calls them...

"Peacemakers who _____ in _____."

And what is the result? They...

"reap a _____ of _____."

James is telling us that a wise person will do everything he or she can to help promote peace.

Think again about your home life. Are you at peace in your heart? Do you seek peace in your relationships with your brothers and sisters? And how about Mom and Dad...do you give them a hard time, or do you make their lives more pleasant, more peaceful?

When you practice heavenly wisdom in your daily actions and conduct, you will please God, promote peace wherever you are, and produce a harvest of righteousness. In other words, you will be doing what's right!

Earthly Wisdom

I probably don't have to tell you that earthly wisdom is the exact opposite of heavenly wisdom! Unfortunately, it's super easy to live by earthly—or human—wisdom. But earthly wisdom will never produce good deeds and humility (verse 13). And earthly wisdom will never produce purity, peace, consideration for others, obedience, mercy, good fruit, impartiality, and sincerity (verse 17).

In verse 14, James tells us what earthly wisdom is hiding in our hearts:

"... bitter _____ and _____ ambition."

These two attitudes come from focusing on what we want for ourselves (selfish ambition) but cannot have (envy). James says at the end of verse 14 that these attitudes might even cause us to...

"boast _____ it [our wordly wisdom] or deny the _____."

Next, James tells us where earthly wisdom actually comes from. Verse 15 says, "Such 'wisdom'...

"does not come _____ from _____ but is earthly, _____, _____."

And now, in verse 16, James reveals what earthly wisdom produces:

"For where you have _____ and _____

_____, there you find _____

and every _____ practice."

James is describing what earthly wisdom looks like in verses 15-16. In verse 15 James gives us two lists. The first list describes the wisdom that "does not come down from heaven." It is...

1. _____

2. _____

3. _____

Just a note: "Earthly" means it considers only the things we can see with our eyes.

"Unspiritual" means it is based on human understanding and is not led by God's Spirit.

"Demonic" means it comes from Satan.

In verse 16, James gives us a second list. He points out the results of the wisdom that does not come down from heaven. He says we will find...

1. _____

2. _____ _____ _____

A picture is worth a thousand words! To see a picture of the damage and harm that envy and selfish ambition can cause, read Numbers 12:1-2 below. As you read, keep in mind that Aaron, Moses, and Miriam were siblings—brothers and sister.

"Miriam and Aaron began to talk against Moses because of his Cushite wife, for he had married a Cushite. 'Has the LORD spoken only through Moses?' they asked. 'Hasn't he also spoken through us?' And the LORD heard this."

Miriam and Aaron wanted to be considered leaders of the nation of Israel just like their brother Moses. They began to complain about Moses and to question his character, his marriage, and his leadership position. This created a horrible conflict in their family. So they spoke against Moses to the people. They were not peacemakers. No, they were troublemakers.

Please don't be jealous or critical of your brother or sister!

Don't live and act according to "earthly wisdom," which is the source of "every evil practice." Instead, focus on doing what's right, on what God wants you to do. Focus on being the best sister you can be—a sister who does the right thing and does not criticise her family members.

My friend, earthly wisdom is not true wisdom at all. It creates tension and trouble wherever you go. Think of it this way:

The world's kind of wisdom should be avoided at all cost.
God's kind of wisdom should be pursued at all cost.

A LOOK INSIDE YOUR HEART

God is growing so many beautiful qualities in your heart! He wants you to focus on the heavenly wisdom He provides. If you do, then as you live your life and your faith in your home and at school and church, these attitudes and actions will cause you to "reap a harvest of righteousness"! You will be a peacemaker rather than a troublemaker.

I love the book of James because he tells it like it is. James uses very simple language so you won't miss God's message. James also creates lists that spell out what attitudes and actions God wants to build in you. He also lets you know what God absolutely does not want to see—those things that are not from Him, but are "demonic," coming from the devil.

As always, look at your heart. What do you see there? Are you producing heavenly or earthly wisdom?

A HEART CHECKUP

We've covered a LOT of information in this chapter. We inspected two different kinds of wisdom—heavenly wisdom and earthly wisdom. We looked at seven characteristics of heavenly wisdom. We definitely have a better understanding of earthly wisdom.

Now it's time to check your heart. Look again at page 73 and review the seven characteristics of heavenly wisdom. Then write down two or three ways you can use the heavenly wisdom God is giving you. When you are done, pray to your heavenly Father and thank Him for His heavenly wisdom. He will delight in helping you to do His will—to do what's right!

"With God's help, I will use heavenly wisdom to...

1. _____

_____

2. _____

_____

3. _____

_____

A PRAYER TO PRAY

"Our father in heaven..." That's You, God! I love praying to You, and I really like praying the Lord's Prayer. I want to thank You with all my heart for the wisdom that is from above—Your perfect, heavenly wisdom that is always available to me. I can pray to You and ask for Your wisdom, and I can read Your Word and find it. Open my heart and my will to want to do what's right...and to do it. I want to show the whole world by what I say and do that I am a true follower of You. Thank You for being my heavenly Father! I love You. Amen.

GEMS FROM JAMES

"Who is wise and understanding among you?
Let them show it by their good life,
by deeds done in the humility
that comes from wisdom."
James 3:13

"Where you have envy and selfish ambition,
there you find disorder and every evil practice."
James 3:16

"The wisdom that comes from heaven
is first of all pure; then peace-loving, considerate,
submissive, full of mercy and good fruit,
impartial and sincere."
James 3:17

Getting Close to God

JAMES 4:1-10

¹ What causes fights and quarrels among you? Don't they come from your desires that battle within you?

² You desire but do not have, so you kill. You covet but you cannot get what you want, so you quarrel and fight. You do not have because you do not ask God.

³ When you ask, you do not receive, because you ask with wrong motives, that you may spend what you get on your pleasures.

⁴ You adulterous people, don't you know that friendship with the world means enmity against God? Therefore, anyone who chooses to be a friend of the world becomes an enemy of God.

⁵ Or do you think Scripture says without reason that he jealously longs for the spirit he has caused to dwell in us?

⁶ But he gives us more grace. That is why Scripture says:

> "God opposes the proud
> but shows favor to the humble."

⁷ Submit yourselves, then, to God. Resist the devil, and he will flee from you.

⁸ Come near to God and he will come near to you. Wash your hands, you sinners, and purify your hearts, you double-minded.

⁹ Grieve, mourn and wail. Change your laughter to mourning and your joy to gloom.

¹⁰ Humble yourselves before the Lord, and he will lift you up.

Oh, dear! Here comes an important topic for you...and me...and everyone on the face of the earth! But before we get into it, here's a little background.

When God created Adam and Eve, everything was perfect. The two of them were close to God. They even walked and talked with Him...that is, until Adam and Eve ate the one fruit God told them not to eat!

At that very second, sin and chaos immediately entered the world. Adam and Eve began moving away from God, and their children continued moving even farther away from God, causing great grief to God and to Adam and Eve. Because of anger, jealousy, hatred, and sibling rivalry, Cain killed his brother Abel, committing the very first murder.

Do you have brothers and sisters? If so, I'm sure you know that brothers and sisters quarrel and argue. Sometimes you even yell and lose your temper. When you live under the same roof with anyone, you will struggle with competition, selfishness, and anger.

Well, James has some really important advice for us. He's got information that will help us understand how we can get closer to God so we can do a better job of getting along with others—especially those at home!

Why is it so hard to get along with people, and what can we do about it? Before we dive into James's answers to these questions, let's take a look at Genesis 4:2-8 and find out exactly what happened between Cain and his brother Abel.

² Now Abel kept flocks, and Cain worked the soil.

³ In the course of time Cain brought some of the fruits of the soil as an offering to the LORD.

⁴ And Abel also brought an offering—fat portions from some of the firstborn of his flock. The LORD looked with favor on Abel and his offering,

⁵ but on Cain and his offering he did not look with favor. So Cain was very angry, and his face was downcast.

⁶ Then the LORD said to Cain, "Why are you angry? Why is your face downcast?

⁷ If you do what is right, will you not be accepted? But if you do not do what is right, sin is crouching at your door; it desires to have you, but you must rule over it."

⁸ Now Cain said to his brother Abel, "Let's go out to the field." While they were in the field, Cain attacked his brother Abel and killed him.

What do verses 4 and 5 say caused Cain to be angry and hate his brother?

"The LORD looked with _____ on Abel and

his _____, but on Cain and his

_____ he _____ _____

look with _____. So Cain was very

_____..."

This is an awful and sad story, right? Cain was not interested in getting near to God or doing what God wanted him to do. So in his anger, Cain did a terrible thing—he killed his brother.

The Downside of Life

As we begin looking at James, chapter 4, prepare yourself to find a list of sins like what we saw in Cain. This list shows us the downside of life, the sins we commit that go against God's Word and keep us from being close to God.

To begin, do you ever wonder, as James asks in verse 1, "What causes fights and quarrels among you?" Write out James's answers in verse 1.

"...they come from your _____ that battle

_____ _____."

Now write the answer James gives in verse 2.

"You desire but _____ _____ have, so you

_____."

James continues in verse 2: "You covet [or long for something]...

but you cannot _____ _____ _____

_____, so you _____ and

_____."

James ends verse 2 by telling us what will help us with envy, jealously, and the desire for what we do not have—things that keep us from getting closer to God.

"You do not have because you _____ _____

_____ _____."

Have you ever prayed and prayed for something, but nothing happened? It's easy to get frustrated and confused when you think God hasn't answered your prayer. James reveals one of the reasons this might happen. What does he say about this in verse 3? "When you ask, you do not receive,

"...because _____ _____ with _____

_____, that you may _____

what _____ _____ on your _____."

If you have a journal, notebook, or diary you love to write in, here are some things you can do. Or you can use page 98.

— Write out your prayer requests. Then take a look at your list and think about what you are really asking for—and why you are asking for it.

— The next time you pray, listen to yourself, your words. What are you really praying for? Are you thinking of others and asking God to help them, or are you thinking of yourself and asking for what you want?

In verses 2 and 3, James names the most common problems in prayer. After listening to yourself pray, check the one—or ones—that describe the content of your prayers.

    ___ I am not asking at all (verse 2).

    ___ I am asking for the wrong reasons (verse 3).

    ___ I am asking for the wrong things (verse 3).

— Try writing out your prayers. Then pray them to God out loud. Hearing what you are actually asking for will help you correct all three of the problems above.

Here's something to think about. I read a story about a boy whose father grew corn and stored massive amounts of it on his farm, waiting for the price of his corn to go up so he could sell it for a great deal of money. Every day the boy's dad prayed, "O God, remember the poor and needy and supply their wants and needs."

One day after his father finished praying this prayer, the boy asked, "Daddy, may I have half of your corn in the barns?" Naturally the dad asked "Why? What would you do with all that corn?"

The boy answered, "I would answer your prayers for the poor and needy. I would give them some corn."[6]

Always remember, God wants us to ask—
to ask for the right things, and
to ask with the right motives.

A Wake-Up Call

James, chapter 4, verses 4-6, is what we could refer to as a wake-up call. Do you want to know if you are getting closer to God...or farther away? James begins in verse 4 by asking,

"...don't you know that _____ with

the _____ means enmity against

_____?"

> **Just a note:** "Enmity" means hostility or ill will or hatred.

What does James conclude in verse 4?

"...anyone who chooses to be a _____ of

the world becomes an _____ of God."

James 4, verse 5, is a little hard to understand. The New Century Version may make James's message a little clearer: "Do you think the Scripture means nothing that says, 'The Spirit that God made to live in us wants us for himself alone'?"

This means that instead of focusing on ourselves and being selfish and worldly, we are to focus on God and the Holy Spirit.

What does it mean to focus on Him? It includes...

Thanking God every day for the Holy Spirit, who lives in all of us who truly believe—in all Christians.

This will help you to remember God is always with you!

Trusting God to meet every one of your needs. When you know that God is taking care of you, you don't need to worry about getting what you want.

Obeying God by loving other people in practical ways. God wants you to bless others.

When we focus on God and thank Him, trust Him, and obey Him, we will soon realize that the things we have been wanting are nothing compared with what God offers us. When this happens, you will know you are getting closer to God!

Don't miss the wonderful truth in verse 6! God is always available to help you do what He wants you to do. He never asks you to do anything that He will not help you accomplish. What does God give you and all His people so we can stand strong against the evil ways of the world?

"...he gives us _____ _____."

God's Divine Checklist

Are you ready for another list from James? James 4:7-10 is a list that includes commands, instructions, and information for drawing nearer to God. It's kind of a "Divine Checklist" for people who want to be friends with God and not friends with the world. As a girl after God's own heart who loves the Lord, drawing nearer to God is what your life is all about. So let's learn more about our relationship with God from James's list. Fill in the blanks with words from the Bible verses. And most of all, open your heart to receive these truths and practice them.

Before we move into God's call to serve Him, James reminds us in verse 6 that the Bible says,

"God opposes the _____ but shows favor

to the _____."

In verse 7, James begins his Divine Checklist for friends of God:

✓ **#1** "Submit _____, then, to

_____."

Just a note: To "submit" means to choose to do things God's way, to yield to God's Word and His will for your life, to follow His directions.

As God's friends, we never have to be afraid of our enemy, the devil. In verse 7, what else does James tell us we should do, and what will be the result?

✓ **#2** "Resist the _____, and he will

_____ from _____."

To resist the devil means to choose *not* to give in to temptation. When you do that, the devil turns away. In verse 8, what happens when you turn to God?

✓ **#3** "Come near to _____ and he will

_____ _____ to _____."

When you come near to God, you are turning away from the devil. You are also turning away from your sins. In verse 8, James says that when we turn away from our sins, it's like we are washing them off of us.

✓ **#4** "Wash _____ _____, you

sinners, and purify _____ _____,

you _____-_____."

As we wash those sins away, we often feel sorry for the things we've done. James describes those feelings in verse 9:

✓ **#5** "Grieve, _____ and _____."

Does this mean we are always supposed to be sad? No way! However, rather than laughing about our poor choices, we are to be serious about turning away from them, as James explains in verse 9:

✓ **#6** "Change your _____

to _____ and your _____ to

_____."

Whew—that's a LOT to think about! Now, in verse 10, James finishes his list the way he started it—with some really great news. Look what happens when we decide to humble ourselves and become friends with God:

✓ **#7** "Humble _____ before

the _____, and he will lift _____

_____."

Isn't that amazing? Think about this: You don't have to lift yourself up—to put yourself first or spend time and energy getting what you want. Instead, when you humble yourself, *God* will lift up! He is a true friend—*your* true friend.

Now, go back through God's Divine Checklist and write below the first word in each of the seven commands given in verses 7-10. These acts and choices will help you grow closer to God.

S _____

R _____

C _____

W _____

G _____

C _____

H _____

A LOOK INSIDE YOUR HEART

The Old Testament book of Proverbs is a lot like the book of James—they are both full of practical instructions for our everyday lives. Much of Proverbs is directed to young men and women. Here's a really key proverb for you: "Above all else, guard your heart, for everything you do flows from it" (Proverbs 4:23).

Your heart is the key to getting close to God. With your heart you love God. With your heart you obey His Word. With your heart you talk to God in prayer. With your heart you make right—or wrong!—choices. With your heart you love others. With your heart you select the words you say—and the words you don't say! With your heart you choose to walk in God's ways, to live out your faith.

In just this one chapter we have seen a LOT of heart action and heart responses. For instance...

— This lesson began with fighting and quarreling. The heart, my friend, is where we choose not to argue and fight. The heart is where we test our motives and the reasons we do or want certain things.

— Another lesson James sent to our hearts is to work on a deep and close relationship with God—not with the world. In fact, James said, "Anyone who chooses to be a friend of the world becomes an enemy of God" (verse 4). So where is your heart? Do you love God...or do you love the world? As you read your Bible each day, God's Word will wash your heart and soul...and lead you to live God's way—to live close to Him.

— Our final lesson was all about humility. There is nothing so beautiful and lovely as a girl with a humble heart. From the heart we submit ourselves to God. With a humble heart we draw near to God. With the heart we joyfully and humbly serve others. And it is the humble heart that will seek to be pure.

As a girl after God's own heart, make a decision each day to follow this instruction we found in the book of Proverbs: "Above all else, guard your heart, for everything you do flows from it." If you are not sure how to get started, do as James advised in verse 2. He wrote, "You do not have because you do not ask God." Become a girl who prays every day. Ask God to help you, to guide you, and to show you the way to His heart— the way to become a girl after God's own heart.

Look at prayer this way: How do you get to know someone at school or in your neighborhood? You talk with them, right? It's the same way with God. Prayer is the way you get closer to Him and know Him better. Prayer is how God becomes your best friend.

A HEART CHECKUP

Here are some exercises you can use to strengthen your heart and your love for God—and they all come from James 4:7-10. These steps will help you grow closer to Him.

- ❤ "Give yourselves humbly to God" (4:7 TLB). Realize that you need God's forgiveness, and be willing to follow him.

- ❤ "Resist the devil" (4:7). You don't have to believe his lies or give in to his temptations.

- ❤ "Wash your hands" (that is, lead a pure life) and "let your hearts be filled with God alone" (4:8 TLB). Be cleansed from sin, and replace it with God's purity.

- ❤ Let there be tears, sorrow, and sincere grief for your sins (4:9).

- ❤ "Humble yourselves before the Lord (4:10)." Recognize that your worth comes from God alone. He will lift you up (1 Peter 5:6).[7]

A PRAYER TO PRAY

O my dear heavenly Father, do I ever have some work to do! As I look into my heart, I see a lot of things that are on Your list of things I am not to do. Right this minute I am humbling myself before You as I pray. I am asking You from my heart to work in my heart, to lead me to good, better, and best choices—choices that draw me closer to You, choices that make me more like You. That's what I want more than anything else. I love You, Father, and I need Your help. Amen.

"You do not have because you do not ask God."
James 4:2

"When you ask, you do not receive, because you ask with wrong motives, that you may spend what you get on your pleasures."
James 4:3

"Anyone who chooses to be a friend of the world becomes an enemy of God."
James 4:4

"God opposes the proud but shows favor to the humble."
James 4:6

Be Careful What You Say

JAMES 4:11-17

11 Brothers and sisters, do not slander one another. Anyone who speaks against a brother or sister or judges them speaks against the law and judges it. When you judge the law, you are not keeping it, but sitting in judgment on it.

12 There is only one Lawgiver and Judge, the one who is able to save and destroy. But you—who are you to judge your neighbor?

13 Now listen, you who say, "Today or tomorrow we will go to this or that city, spend a year there, carry on business and make money."

14 Why, you do not even know what will happen tomorrow. What is your life? You are a mist that appears for a little while and then vanishes.

15 Instead, you ought to say, "If it is the Lord's will, we will live and do this or that."

16 As it is, you boast in your arrogant schemes. All such boasting is evil.

17 If anyone, then, knows the good they ought to do and doesn't do it, it is sin for them.

Oh, boy! Watch out! James is diving into deep water, and he isn't holding anything back. He's got a handful of urgent things to say—and we've got some choices to make. His messages are so important that he can't wait to tell us. And he cannot gently work his way up to sharing these truths. No, he's got to tell us NOW! So here we go!

Choose to Bless

Right away, in James 4, verse 11, what does James want us to know? "Brothers and sisters,

do not _____

_____ another."

> **Just a note:** "Slander" is a word that means...
> — to smear someone's reputation
> — to falsely accuse or charge someone with something that is not true.

You and I—and everyone—have had experiences when we slandered someone, or when we were the ones who were slandered. And we know from personal experience that slander or gossip hurts. It hurts our feelings. It hurts our reputation. It hurts our friendships. And worst of all, it hurts our testimony and reputation as a Christian, as a person who knows God.

And there's more harm done: When we gossip and slander others, it's like taking a step backward in our journey of becoming a girl after God's own heart. But we can thank God that when we make bad choices, we can confess those sins to Him, and He will make us clean again.

As you continue reading, realize this is not the first or last time God's people are told not to gossip about others or slander others. The Old Testament law tells us,

> "Do not go about spreading slander among your people" (Leviticus 19:16).

Also, one of the Ten Commandments states,

> "You shall not give false testimony against your neighbor" (Exodus 20:16).

Gossip and slander are real problems for most girls—whether they are young like you or old like your grandmother! Why do we gossip? Maybe we really enjoy sharing secrets with a best friend. Maybe we want some attention—which we definitely get when we are sharing juicy bits of gossip. Maybe we want to feel like we are better than someone else, so we put them down or share something bad or embarrassing or untrue about them.

Here in God's Word, James is telling you, "Do not slander one another." He is asking you to choose to be a girl after God's own heart—to choose to be a girl who blesses others, a girl who builds people up instead of tearing them down with gossip and slander. If gossip is a problem for you, here are some things you can do.

Things to Do to Conquer Gossip

- ❤ Give your tongue back to God! He made it, and He'd like to help you control it.

- ❤ Ask God to forgive you for the times you've listened to or repeated gossip.

- ❤ Think of something you can say whenever your friends start to gossip. ("Can we talk about something else?")[8]

Choose to Love

You have probably noticed that in his letter to people like you and me, James talks a lot about love. He also tells us about a lot of actions and attitudes that do not show love. Here in verses 11 and 12 he writes,

"Anyone who _____ against a _____ or _____ or judges _____ speaks against the _____ and _____ _____."

In the same verse, James continues,

"When you _____ the law, you are not _____ _____, but _____ in _____ on _____."

In verse 12, James explains, "There is only one Lawgiver and Judge, the one who is able to save and destroy." Then James asks,

"But you—who _____ _____ to judge

_____ _____?"

James is pointing out that God is the Lawgiver and Judge. And God is telling us in His Word that we are absolutely not to slander. He is also telling us that when we judge and criticize someone, when we put down and belittle others by our slander, we are actually judging and criticizing God's law of love. No wonder God wonders, "But you—who are you to judge your neighbor?" It's like He is asking, "Just who do you think you are!"

You and I were not put on this earth to judge others. That's God's job. But God makes it super clear that we *are* put on this earth to love others. So let your love flow! Let it shine!

What can help us stop criticizing and putting down other people? Check out these solutions from the Bible—and check two or three of them you want to remember...and practice.

_____ "Do to others what you would have them do to you" (Matthew 7:12).

_____ "Love your neighbor as you love yourself" (Matthew 22:39).

_____ "This is my command: Love each other" (John 15:17).

_____ "Over all these virtues put on love" (Colossians 3:14).

_____ "Love the family of believers" (1 Peter 2:17).

_____ "Let us love one another, for love comes from God" (1 John 4:7).

_____ "He has given us this command: Anyone who loves God must also love their brother and sister" (1 John 4:21).

Here's a girly thing to think about. In the list above my eyes went straight to Colossians 3:14, which says, "Over all these virtues put on love." When I saw this my mind immediately went to the routine of getting dressed each day.

Here's the picture. You know the drill: You've got clothes in a closet and in drawers. (Well, at least I hope they are in a closet and in some drawers, and not thrown all over the floor, bed, and furniture!) Anyway, each day you get dressed. You select and put on clothes. And of course, you like some of your clothes better than others. You have favorite colors, favorite styles...and favorite shoes! And maybe you slip on a favorite necklace or bracelet or headband.

Now think about this—every time you dress, pick the clothes you like and make sure you have your mom's approval. Then get dressed. But before you walk out of your room, be sure to "put on love." Then go through your day spreading God's love everywhere you go. Choose to love, and refuse to gossip or slander others. And refuse to be with those who do. Your homework assignment from God is to love.

Choose to Trust God

James has been showing us one problem with the way we talk—we hurt other people when we say bad things about them. Now he shows us another problem with our words, and it has to do with the way we make our plans.

Travel is not something new. In James's day (about 50 AD,

which was almost 2000 years ago!), people didn't travel by jet airplanes and cars. Instead, salesmen traveled from city to city in caravans and on ships.

Evidently these men were quite the planners! Maybe that's because their tedious journeys—trekking through dry desert lands and sailing across seas—often took up to a year. Read now in James 4:13 how James begins a message about trusting God with our plans.

> "Now listen, you who say, 'Today or tomorrow we will go to this or that city, spend a year there, carry on business and make money.'"

With all their planning, these business people were forgetting a few facts of life! In verse 14, James reminds them,

> "...you do not even know what _____ _____
>
> _____. What is _____
>
> _____? You are a _____ that
>
> appears for a _____ _____ and
>
> then _____."

These people were bragging about how they would spend their time and live their lives and earn money, but James tells them in verse 15,

> "Instead, you ought to say, 'If it is the _____
>
> _____, we will _____ and do _____
>
> or _____.'"

James points out their arrogance in verse 16:

"As it is, you boast in your _____

_____. All such _____

is _____."

In verses 14-16, James told these merchants—and all of God's people—to remember God and honor Him in all that they do, including their planning.

> **Just a note**: God is not asking you to stop planning or stop moving forward toward solid goals. But God is reminding you that He is in full control. Everything in your life should be approached with this mindset: "If it is the Lord's will…" (verse 15). You are to acknowledge and consider God in all your planning and activities.

Now, in verse 17, James wraps up his message with a key principle for living the Christian life: "If anyone, then, knows…

the _____ they ought to _____ and

_____ do it, it is _____

_____ _____."

In James 3:9 we learned that "with the tongue we praise our Lord and Father, and with it we curse human beings, who have been made in God's likeness." Well, my friend, what comes out of your mouth is a matter of the heart. Jesus said "the mouth speaks what the heart is full of" (Luke 6:45). When we slander someone and hurt or ruin their reputation, we are showing the whole watching world what's going on in our heart and mind, and it's not very pretty.

What can you do about your heart? Start by filling your heart and mind with God's Word each morning—before you step out of your room and your home.

God's Word will also teach you about love—and how to love. While you are alone with God, think about Him. Pray to Him. Thank and praise Him. Seek to please Him—to be a girl after God's own heart, a girl who wants to love Him, obey Him, trust Him, and do His will—a girl who lives her faith.

In this chapter we also learned that all our plans should include God. We are "stewards"—or managers—of our time. That means our time is really His, and we are to use it the way He wants us to. God wants us to be open to His will. He wants us to plan our time and activities around Him, with Him in mind. It's sort of a Plan A–Plan B mentality. You work on Plan A while being open to any change in your day God wants to make.

Let's say you are supposed to go shopping with Mom today (that's your Plan A), but something comes up and she can't go. Because you have given your day to God and you trust Him to lead you through it, you don't have a fit. You don't pout. You don't complain. You don't lock yourself into your room and cry. No, you roll with it! You accept God's plan—Plan B—which is always best. As James said in verse 15, when we make our plans, we say, "If it is the Lord's will, we will...do this or that."

When you make your plans or set your eye on something, make sure you remain flexible so you can turn whenever and wherever God leads you. Let the desire of your heart always be to do what God wants you to do—and He will let you know His plan, which will always be "his good, pleasing and perfect will" (Romans 12:2).

A HEART CHECKUP

Now let's take the information from your **Look Inside Your Heart** and use it for your **Heart Checkup.** Ask yourself...

- ❤ How often did I gossip last week? (Circle one.)

  every day   several times   not too much at all

- ❤ What one thing will I do each day to stop this sin?

  _____

  _____

- ❤ About how often am I filling my mind and heart with God's Word? (Circle one.)

  every day   several times a week   only at church

❤ Write out what you plan to do next week to fill your heart with God's truths.

_____

_____

❤ How do I usually handle a Plan B—a change of plans? (Circle one.)

get upset   sulk in my room   accept it as God's will

❤ What one thing will I do to trust God and start being more aware of His will and His plan for my days?

_____

_____

A PRAYER TO PRAY

Father of all that is good, Your Word has reached into my heart, and I realize I need to watch my mouth. You tell me not to gossip or slander. And You tell me not to brag about all my big plans. I need to think of You more often—like, all the time!—so I will use my mouth to bless others instead of slander them. I want You to be at the heart of all my plans, and I trust You to lead me. Help me to know and do—and speak—what is good. I love You, Father God! Sooo much! Amen.

"Brothers and sisters, do not slander one another."
James 4:11

"Who are you to judge your neighbor?"
James 4:12

"What is your life?
You are a mist that appears for a little while
and then vanishes."
James 4:14

"You ought to say, 'If it is the Lord's will,
we will live and do this or that.'"
James 4:15

"If anyone, then, knows the good
they ought to do and doesn't do it,
it is sin for them."
James 4:17

Living Your Faith

What's in Your Heart?

JAMES 5:1-9

1 Now listen, you rich people, weep and wail because of the misery that is coming on you.

2 Your wealth has rotted, and moths have eaten your clothes.

3 Your gold and silver are corroded. Their corrosion will testify against you and eat your flesh like fire. You have hoarded wealth in the last days.

4 Look! The wages you failed to pay the workers who mowed your fields are crying out against you. The cries of the harvesters have reached the ears of the Lord Almighty.

5 You have lived on earth in luxury and self-indulgence. You have fattened yourselves in the day of slaughter.

6 You have condemned and murdered the innocent one, who was not opposing you.

7 Be patient, then, brothers and sisters, until the Lord's coming. See how the farmer waits for the land to yield

its valuable crop, patiently waiting for the autumn and spring rains.

⁸ You too, be patient and stand firm, because the Lord's coming is near.

⁹ Don't grumble against one another, brothers and sisters, or you will be judged. The Judge is standing at the door!

A quick look at online studies reveals how girls choose to spend their money. Would you believe food (including Starbucks) was up at the top? This favorite category is followed by clothes, makeup, and accessories. Yes, this is sounding like us girls!

Have you ever saved any money in a piggy bank at home or a savings account at a bank? Maybe your parents give you an allowance. Maybe they have a list of chores you can do at home to earn extra money. Maybe you have other jobs, like taking care of people's pets while they're on vacation or helping them vacuum or dust their houses. Maybe you bake homemade chocolate chip cookies and have a lemonade and cookie stand in your neighborhood driveway. Maybe you sell crafts or jewelry you've made. Maybe you even get birthday or Christmas money from your grandparents...Sweet!

There are a lot of ways you can earn money. Just be sure to get your parents' permission and advice before you spend it!

Having some money means you also have some responsibilities and decisions to make about what to do with your money. In James, chapter 5, James has a very important and practical message for us about money and our heart. Just read the first two words of verse 1. You will definitely get the picture of how urgent James's message is going to be. Write them in the blanks below, and then let's learn a few things about what God says about money and your heart.

"_____ _____"

Guard Your Heart

James gets our attention when he writes, "Now listen..." That definitely sounds like he wants to give us a wake-up call! James is addressing people who have more money than they need to live each day. He is not condemning them for having money, but he is condemning them for misusing their money. He is telling these "rich people" to straighten up and listen to an urgent warning. This is his message in verse 1:

"Now listen, you _____ people, _____

and _____ because of the _____

that is coming _____ _____."

In verses 2 and 3, James delivers the first message he has for wealthy people who hoarded their money:

"Your wealth has _____, and moths

have _____ your _____.

Your _____ and _____ are

_____."

In a minute we'll return to verse 3, but for now let's look at several truths Jesus spoke in Matthew 6:19-20. First, Jesus tells us what *not* to do.

> "Do not store up for yourselves treasures on earth, where moths and vermin destroy, and where thieves break in and steal" (verse 19).

Just a note: Here, to "store up" means to hoard or save more than you need. People usually do this because they are worried, afraid, or greedy.

Look again at Matthew 6:19 and underline Jesus' command. Then write out two ways verse 19 says we can lose what "treasures" or money or things we have:

"where _____ and _____ destroy, and where _____ _____ _____ and _____"

Next, Jesus tells us what we should do.

> "But store up for yourselves treasures in heaven, where moths and vermin do not destroy, and where thieves do not break in and steal" (Matthew 6:20).

Jesus wants us to focus our hearts on heaven, not on earth, where our worldly treasures are. He wants us to know that everything we have on earth will one day be gone, and those earthly things cannot do anything for us in eternity, in heaven. The truth is, we won't even need those earthly treasures in heaven!

Then Jesus gives us a principle to live by in Matthew 6:21:

"For where your treasure is, there your heart will be also."

In other words, if your treasure is in heaven, that's where your heart will be!

Just a note: It's not wrong to make money or have money. In fact, there are many commands in the Bible that tell us to work hard, take care of our family's needs, earn money, use it wisely, and give to the poor. But we are definitely *not* to love money.

Whatever money you have, you are responsible for its use. You have decisions to make about what to do with your money. The Bible says, you need to...

- ❤ Manage it—know where your money comes from and where it goes.

- ❤ Give some of it at church.

- ❤ Keep your eyes, ears, and heart open to good causes and to people in need.

- ❤ Save some of it.

- Spend some of it—for gifts, for something special you've saved up for.

- Include your parents in your plans and decisions. They have years of wisdom and experience in managing money. They have probably even learned a few things the hard way and will be happy to guide and guard you.[9]

Guard Against Greed

Now, back to James as he moves to another topic in James 5, verse 4. Evidently these wealthy people were not paying their workers! They had the money, but instead of giving their employees their wages or salary, these rich people were keeping the money for themselves. In verse 4 James gives the *wages* a voice.

"The wages you failed to _____ the _____ who _____ your fields are _____ _____ _____ you."

Then James refers in verse 4 to the voices of the *workers*:

"The cries of the _____ have reached the _____ of the _____ _____."

Here's a sad summary of what happened to the poor who did not get paid. This will help you understand the seriousness of the sin the wealthy were committing against the poor.

"The defenseless people James mentions here are probably poor laborers. The poor who could not pay their debts were thrown in prison or forced to sell all their possessions, and at times, even sell their family members into slavery. With no opportunity to work off their debts, poor people often died of starvation."[10]

Proverbs 3:27-28 has these instructions for us to remember when it comes to letting go of our money:

"Do not withhold good from those to whom it is due,
    when it is in your power to act.
Do not say to your neighbor,
    'Come back tomorrow and I'll give it to you'—
    when you already have it with you."

Guard Against Worry

After scolding the wealthy for mistreating their poor workers, James has a message from his heart to share with those who are poor and suffering.

Verse 7:

"Be patient, then, brothers and sisters, until the _____

_____. See how the farmer waits for

the _____ to yield its _____

_____, patiently _____ for the

_____ and _____ rains."

Verse 8:

"You too, be patient and _____ _____,
because the _____ _____
is near."

Verse 9:

"Don't _____ against _____
_____, brothers and sisters, or you
_____ be _____. The Judge is
_____ at the _____!"

What does James tell those who are poor and suffering to do in verse 7?

"Be _____"

What does James tell the poor to do in verse 8?

"Be _____ _____
_____ _____."

In verse 7, how long does James encourage those who are suffering to be patient?

"...until the _____ _____"

And in verse 8, what reason does James give for them to be patient and stand firm?

"...the _____ _____ is

_____."

In five words, what does James tell those who are suffering *not* to do in verse 9?

"Don't _____ _____

_____ _____."

Here's a fact of life to remember. Jesus said it: "In this world you will have trouble" (John 16:33). These poor workers had trouble—and so will you. They worried—and so will you. Are you wondering how you can make it through your trouble and hard times and painful problems? Do as James instructed:

Be patient.
Stand firm.
Don't grumble against each other.

When you are worrying about your day and your troubles and your problems, remember how Jesus ended John 16:33: "But take heart! I have overcome the world."

A LOOK INSIDE YOUR HEART

I really like what Jesus said about the heart in Matthew 6:21. I've even memorized it:

"Where your treasure is, there your heart will be also."

God gives us all kinds of treasure. Just think about it—He gives you loving parents, a family, a place to live, and the opportunity to go to school and get an education. You probably have enough food, some friends, and even some hobbies! In school you are learning and growing as you prepare for the future.

As you have seen in this chapter, money is very low on God's list of things you must, must, must have! In your heart, focus instead on what you already have. Give thanks from your heart to God for how He has blessed you. Pray from your heart each day—and often through the day—for your challenges and for others. And open your heart as you live in a world where most people have less than you have.

A HEART CHECKUP

Do you struggle with giving some of your money at church? If you're like most people, at first you don't want to give. Then you begin to realize that you should. I read an article for girls that said you are to be a good steward of the money you have today—even if that is only $3.52 in your piggy bank! If this describes you, then the next time you go to church, start with giving 10 percent—what is often referred to as a "tithe"—even if that's only 35 cents.

Here's a checklist that can help you see what is—or isn't—in your purse…and your heart.

___ Tithe religiously.

___ Give freely.

___ Spend cautiously.

___ Save abundantly.

___ Invest carefully.

___ Budget regularly.[11]

Check any items you need to get started on or need to improve on right away.

A PRAYER TO PRAY

Jesus, I know in my heart I would really like to have more money! But thank You for teaching me that what money I have, I must take care of and use carefully. Help me to be a hard worker, to give to my church, to be aware of the poor, to spoil my brothers and sisters with little surprise gifts (and of course, Mom and Dad too!) and to think—and pray—before I spend my money. In my heart I want to be someone who gives other people love and encouragement—and money. As You said, where my treasure is, there my heart will be also. I want it to be with You, Jesus, and I want to be like You! I love You. Amen.

"Be patient...until the Lord's coming."
James 5:7

"Be patient and stand firm,
because the Lord's coming is near."
James 5:8

"Don't grumble against one another."
James 5:9

Becoming a Girl After God's Own Heart

JAMES 5:10-20

10 Brothers and sisters, as an example of patience in the face of suffering, take the prophets who spoke in the name of the Lord.

11 As you know, we count as blessed those who have persevered. You have heard of Job's perseverance and have seen what the Lord finally brought about. The Lord is full of compassion and mercy.

12 Above all, my brothers and sisters, do not swear—not by heaven or by earth or by anything else. All you need to say is a simple "Yes" or "No." Otherwise you will be condemned.

13 Is anyone among you in trouble? Let them pray. Is anyone happy? Let them sing songs of praise.

14 Is anyone among you sick? Let them call the elders of the church to pray over them and anoint them with oil in the name of the Lord.

¹⁵ And the prayer offered in faith will make the sick person well; the Lord will raise them up. If they have sinned, they will be forgiven.

¹⁶ Therefore confess your sins to each other and pray for each other so that you may be healed. The prayer of a righteous person is powerful and effective.

¹⁷ Elijah was a human being, even as we are. He prayed earnestly that it would not rain, and it did not rain on the land for three and a half years.

¹⁸ Again he prayed, and the heavens gave rain, and the earth produced its crops.

¹⁹ My brothers and sisters, if one of you should wander from the truth and someone should bring that person back,

²⁰ remember this: Whoever turns a sinner from the error of their way will save them from death and cover over a multitude of sins.

Have you ever watched a TV program that began with the words, "Previously on..."? These words are then followed by a brief review of what happened on the previous episode. Your teachers probably do the same thing. They often begin their classes with a review of what you have already learned before they start into new material.

Well, my friend, let's review what has been happening in James 5, and then we will move forward with new material. "Previously," in James 5:1-9,

— James talked to us about money.

— James was especially upset that those with money were not paying their workers.

— James told the rich people they were sinning against the poor.

— James encouraged the poor workers to be patient, not to give up—and not to grumble and quarrel against each other. Why? Read on!

— James explained: Because the Lord is coming. "The Lord's coming is near." Indeed, "The Judge is standing at the door" (James 5:7-9). Instead of worrying, those who were suffering were to be patient and trust God.

Be Anxious for Nothing

You already know James loves to illustrate the truths he is sharing with his readers—and with us! After telling those who were suffering to be patient, James gave several examples of people who suffered with patience. He wanted these examples to encourage and strengthen those who had to stand up and endure great stress. Using the Bible verses, fill in these blanks:

The example in verse 10: "Brothers and sisters, as an example of patience in the face of suffering,

take the _____ who spoke in the

_____ of the _____."

The example in verse 11: "You have heard of...

_____ _____ and

have seen what the _____ finally

_____ _____."

What do you learn about the Lord in verse 11?

"The Lord is _____ of _____

and _____."

God's prophets suffered...and patiently persevered through their suffering. Job suffered...and he, too, patiently persevered through his suffering. When you are suffering, remember that those who have gone before you suffered. Draw courage from their examples of faith and endurance. With God's help and grace, you, too, can patiently persevere through your difficult times.

Be Careful What You Say

"Previously" in James, chapter 5, James told those who were suffering to...

— be patient (verse 8),

— stand firm (verse 8), and

— do not grumble against one another (verse 9).

Now James continues his advice to those who are suffering. In verse 12, He tells them,

"...do not _____ —not by _____
or by _____ or by _____
_____."

Instead of swearing on something or by something, James says in verse 12,

"All you need to say is a _____

'_____' or '_____.'"

Have you ever heard someone say, "I swear to God"? I've even heard people say, "I swear on a stack of Bibles" or "I swear on my mother's grave." Well, this is exactly what James does not want believers in Christ to do. All we are to say is "Yes" or "No" to the questions we receive. One Bible teacher gives this advice:

"Always be honest so that others will believe your simple 'yes' or 'no.' By avoiding lies, half-truths, and omissions of the truth, you will become known as a trustworthy person."[12]

Just a note: What James is telling us goes all the way back to the Ten Commandments. The third commandment says, "You shall not misuse the name of the LORD your God, for the LORD will not hold anyone guiltless who misuses his name" (Exodus 20:7).

Be Faithful to Pray

I love to study the Bible, but I always have to ask, "So what? How can these truths change my life? What do I need to do to practice these truths, to live by faith?"

That's why I really like the way James ends his letter, the book of James. James was an extremely practical man—and by now you know the book of James is an extremely practical book. As the same Bible scholar wrote, the book of James "spells out what it means to follow Jesus day by day."[13] Now, that's practical!

James's instructions are filled with simple wisdom. There are lots of examples in the book of James that help us understand what he is teaching. And there are lots of lists telling us exactly what to do—and not to do.

As you move through the rest of his letter, write out James's instructions in these blanks:

Verse 13: "Is anyone among you in trouble?"

"Let them _____."

Verse 13: "Is anyone happy?"

"Let them _____ _____ of _____."

Verse 14: "Is anyone among you sick?"

"Let them call the _____ of the _____ to _____ _____ _____ and

_____ _____ with _____

in the _____ of the _____."

Be sure you read verse 15 for the exciting results of the ministry of "the prayer offered in faith" and the tender loving care given to those who are sick!

Are you getting God's message? You are to be faithful to pray!

In a final list, James writes in verse 16,

"...confess _____ _____ to _____

_____ and _____ for _____

_____."

Why would we pray for each other? James tell us in verse 16:

"The _____ of a _____

person is _____ and

_____."

Look again at the blanks you filled in for verses 13-16 and circle the words "pray" and "prayer" each time they are used. Do you realize how important your prayer life is? In these four verses, verses 13–16, prayer is a part of the answer to every problem listed.

♥ Is anyone in trouble? Let them pray.

- Is anyone happy? Let them sing songs of praise, which is another form of prayer.

- Is anyone sick? Call for the elders to pray.

- Has anyone sinned? Pray for them.

In verse 10 James told us, "As an example of patience in the face of suffering, take the prophets who spoke in the name of the Lord." Well, now in verse 17 James does just that. He uses the prophet Elijah as another example of powerful and effective prayer. How is Elijah described?

"Elijah was a _____ _____, even as _____ _____."

What did Elijah pray for?

"...that it _____ _____ _____"

What happened?

"...it did _____ _____ on the _____ for _____ and a _____ _____."

When Elijah prayed again, what happened (verse 18)?

"...the heavens _____ _____, and the earth _____ its _____."

Pray, my friend! Present yourself to God each morning and pray for your heart and your day. Pray to be God's girl, a girl after His own heart. Keep a list of people who need your prayers. And keep a constant conversation going with God. Think of every breath you take in as an opportunity to exhale out a prayer to Him. Keep in mind the joy you will have as you talk to God.

Be Aware of Others

James ends his letter begging Christians to watch over other Christians—to practice Christian love. It's easy to be selfish and self-centered. These sins come naturally. As the saying goes, "I'm looking out for number one"—for myself! But being aware of others comes from the heart—a heart that abides in Jesus' love and focuses Jesus' love on others. In verse 19, what are we to do when a Christian we know falls into sin? We should try to

"...bring _____ _____

_____"

One study Bible explains, "We can do this by taking the initiative, praying for the person, and acting in love to meet the person where he is and bring him back to God."[14]

A LOOK INSIDE YOUR HEART

Being a girl after God's own heart is all about your heart. Your heart of love will notice when a friend is struggling. Your heart of love will care enough to start praying for that friend. And your heart of love will want to find out what to do to help that friend. Be sure to talk with your parents about your concerns for your friends. Your parents will have wisdom to share with you and sound advice for you to follow. And they can pray for your friend too!

As the book of James closes, he tells us in the final verse, "Remember this: Whoever turns a sinner from the error of their way will save them from death and cover over a multitude of sins." What a blessing to love and help one another to stay close to God!

A HEART CHECKUP

Take a quick trip back through this lesson and the messages James sends your way. Then pray and ask God, "Am I growing in these godly qualities? Am I...

— being anxious for nothing?

— being careful what I say?

— being faithful to pray?

— being aware of the needs of others?"

You will know you are following after God's own heart when...

...instead of being anxious, you experience the peace of God that passes all understanding (Philippians 4:6-7).

... instead of blurting out words that harm and hurt people, your speech is filled with grace, encouraging others (Colossians 4:6).

...instead of forgetting to pray, you pray faithfully, frequently, and fervently (James 5:16).

...instead of ignoring or overlooking others, you love and honor them (Romans 12:10).

Now go back through "A Heart Checkup" and choose one quality or practice you want to work on this week.

A PRAYER TO PRAY

*Lord of all mercy and compassion, I love thinking about You and praying to You. I have to admit that after going through my **Heart Checkup** and finishing this book, I realize I need to start my spiritual makeover right away...and start it with prayer. Prayer every morning and prayer all day long. You are with me always, so I can always talk to You. And I thank You, Lord, that I can always count on Your help as I talk things over with You. I want to be a girl after Your own heart, to follow You all of my days and walk in all of Your ways. Help me to be Your girl at home and when I'm around other girls. I want to be a blessing to You and to the people in my life. I want everyone to know that You are my best forever friend and that I belong to You. I love You, Lord! Amen.*

"The Lord is full of compassion and mercy."
James 5:11

"Above all...do not swear—not by heaven
or by earth or by anything else.
All you need to say is a simple 'Yes' or 'No.'"
James 5:12

"The prayer of a righteous person
is powerful and effective."
James 5:16

Your Journey with Jesus

Wow, what a trip! I can't believe all the things we've talked about on our journey through the book of James. I truly hope you've enjoyed our adventure. I know I have!

As we've traveled along, we've looked at some of the key areas of a girl's life. We've also discussed what it means to be a girl after God's own heart, a girl who knows God and wants to do His will—to live out her faith.

Before we go our separate ways, I have one really, really important thing to share with you. Did you notice throughout this book we've talked a lot about God and about being a Christian? Maybe you've been wondering, "What does it mean to be a Christian? Am I a Christian? How can I become a Christian?"

By now you are probably not surprised to know that the Bible tells us how to have a personal relationship with God through His Son, Jesus. It also gives us some very basic information. Here are a few verses that are often called "The Romans Road." Every verse is from the book of Romans in the New Testament of the Bible.

The Romans Road

Romans 3:23 tells you about your sinful condition. "For all have sinned and fall short of the glory of God."

Romans 6:23 shows you the result of your sinful condition and reveals the gift God offers to you instead. "The wages of sin is death, but the gift of God is eternal life in Christ Jesus our Lord."

Romans 5:8 points out God's grace and love for you and Christ's solution to your sinful condition. "God demonstrates his own love for us in this: While we were still sinners, Christ died for us."

Romans 10:9-10 reveals some steps to take to become a Christian. "If you declare with your mouth, 'Jesus is Lord,' and believe in your heart that God raised him from the dead, you will be saved."

I meet girls—and women—all the time who are not sure they are Christians. They want to be Christians but don't know how. I have to say, I wondered the same thing! No one shared this information with me until I was 28 years old!

The way to become a Christian is to receive Jesus Christ as your personal Savior. If being God's child and being a Christian is the desire of your heart, you can pray a sincere prayer from your heart like this one:

A Prayer to Pray

God, I want to be Your child, a true girl after Your heart—a girl who lives her life in You, through You, and for You, not for myself. I admit that I sin and often fail to do what You say is right. I receive Your Son, Jesus Christ, into my needy heart. I thank You that He died on the cross for my sins. Thank You for giving me Your grace and Your strength so I can follow You with all my heart. Amen.

You will continue to walk with Jesus throughout your life. You'll be continuing your journey with Jesus and growing more and more like Him as the years pass. For instance...

- ❤ **You are going to grow in faith.** In your Bible, you will get to know more about God and what He wants you to be and do as you live out your faith in Him.

- ❤ **You are going to grow in love**—love for Jesus, love for your family, and love for others.

- ❤ **You are going to grow in the knowledge of God's Word** as you read your Bible, go to church, and surround yourself with friends who love Jesus too.

- ❤ **You are going to grow in wisdom** so you don't make too many mistakes. You'll learn what's right and what's wrong and make wise choices as you read your Bible and talk with your parents and other Christians.

- **You will grow in God's grace** as you hit road-blocks or speed bumps along the way and experience trials. But praise God—His grace is sufficient to see you through and teach you how to handle your problems.

- **You will grow in joy** as you fall more and more in love with Jesus and walk closely with Him. The joy of the Lord will strengthen you for every challenge. And you will know real joy as God rewards you for every victory, accomplishment, and achievement you experience by His grace.

God has great plans for you. Finishing this book is just one step toward discovering His plan. So congratulations on completing this part of the journey to becoming a girl after God's own heart! Keep on living out your faith. Your adventure has only just begun!

Notes

1. Youth for Christ, *Life Application Bible* (Wheaton: Tyndale House, 1988), p. 1917.

2. Grant R. Osborne, ed., *James (Life Application Bible Commentary)* (Wheaton; Tyndale House, 1992), pp. 22-23.

3. Robert Whipple, "Favoritism Is a Huge Problem," *Leadergrow*, https://leadergrow.com/articles/43-favoritism-is-a-huge-problem.

4. Osborne, *James*, p. 52.

5. "Unfair Judges" in *God's Words of Life for Teens* (Grand Rapids, MI: Zondervan, 2000), p. 15.

6. Adapted from M.R. DeHaan and H.G. Bosch, *Our Daily Bread* (Grand Rapids, MI: Zondervan, 1959), December 26.

7. Adapted from Youth for Christ, *Life Application Bible*, p. 1922.

8. Adapted from *Checklist for Life for Teens* (Nashville, TN: Thomas Nelson Publishers, 2002), p. 33.

9. See 1 Corinthians 4:2; 2 Corinthians 9:7; Galatians 2:10; Ephesians 6:1-2.

10. Youth for Christ, *Life Application Bible*, p. 1924.

11. *Checklist for Life for Teens*, p. 248.

12. Osborne, *James*, p. 136.

13. Osborne, *James*, p. 146.

14. Youth for Christ, *Life Application Bible*, p. 1925.

More Great Books for Tween Girls
by Elizabeth George

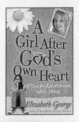

A Girl After God's Own Heart
Learn about building friendships, talking with your parents, putting Jesus first, handling school-work and activities, deciding how to dress, and more. You'll discover how to establish healthy guidelines that honor God, promote your well-being, and help you enjoy life.

A Girl After God's Own Heart Devotional
Your journey with God is the most important jour-ney you will ever take. These heartfelt devotions will help you learn valuable life lessons and draw closer to God.

A Girl's Guide to Making Really Good Choices
You are bombarded with confusing messages about what it means to be a girl. This book will guide you through the most challenging deci-sions you face and help you see that the very best choice of all is a choice to live within God's will.

You Always Have a Friend in Jesus for Girls
Silly jokes, shared interests, laughter and giggles, and whispered dreams—best friends truly *get* each other. And your best friend of all—Jesus— truly *gets* you!

To learn more about Harvest House books
or to read sample chapters, visit our website:

www.HarvestHousePublishers.com

HARVEST HOUSE PUBLISHERS
EUGENE, OREGON